The month of June, from the illuminated manuscript *Les Trés Riches Heures du duc de Berry*

The Story of a Special Day
Volume 158

June

6

157th day of the year
(158th in leap years)
208 days remaining
until the end of the year.

by Michael Dobson

Timespinner
Press

Table of Contents

Cover: The cover photograph, titled "Into the Jaws of Death—US Troops Wading Through Water and Nazi Gunfire," was taken on June 6, 1944 by Chief Photographer's Mate Robert F. Sargent. It shows an LCVP from the US Coast Guard vessel USS *Samuel Chase* disembarking troops of Company E, 16th Infantry, 1st Infantry Division, onto Omaha Beach on the morning of June 6, 1944. Two-thirds of Company E became casualties during the initial landing.

Patrick Henry making his "Give me liberty or give me death!"
speech before the Virginia House of Burgesses, March 23, 1775.
Detail from an 1851 painting by Peter F. Rothermel

June 6 Quotations

"The greater the effort, the greater the glory." ("Plus l'effort est grand, plus la gloire en est grande.")
> — *Pierre Corneille, playwright, born June 6, 1606*

"I regret I have but one life to give for my country."
> — *Nathan Hale, soldier and spy, born June 6, 1755*

"The illusion which exalts us is dearer to us than ten thousand truths."
> — *Александр Пушкин (Aleksandr Pushkin), Russian poet and author, born June 6 [O.S. May 26], 1799*

"I know not what course others may take; but as for me, give me liberty or give me death!"
> — *Patrick Henry, American founding father, died June 6, 1799*

"Create all the happiness you are able to create: remove all the misery you are able to remove."
> — *Jeremy Bentham, philosopher, died June 6, 1832*

"We are most likely to get angry and excited in our opposition to some idea when we ourselves are not quite certain of our own position, and are inwardly tempted to take the other side."
> — *Thomas Mann, writer and Nobel laureate, born June 6, 1875*

"The life of man today is corroded and made bitter by fear. Fear of the future, fear of the hydrogen bomb, fear of ideologies. Perhaps this fear is a greater danger than the danger itself, because it is fear which drives men to act foolishly, to act thoughtlessly, to act dangerously."

— Sukarno, Indonesian president, born June 6, 1901

"My father was a proctologist; my mother was an abstract artist. That's how I view the world."

— Sandra Bernhard, comedienne and actress, born June 6, 1955

"Man needs difficulties; they are necessary for health."

— Carl Jung, psychiatrist, died June 6, 1961

"Every society gets the kind of criminal it deserves. What is equally true is that every community gets the kind of law enforcement it insists on."

— Robert F. Kennedy, US Senator and presidential candidate, died June 6, 1968

Event of the Day
D-Day

On June 6, 1944, a force of 156,000 Allied soldiers, sailors, and airmen began the invasion of Normandy, France, to gain a foothold on the European mainland and eventually wrest Europe from Nazi control. This was known as Operation Overlord, but is best known as D-Day.

US Troops disembarking on Utah Beach, June 6, 1944.

Attacking five separate beachheads heavily defended by some 50,000 German troops, the Allies encountered withering fire and numerous obstacles. On the first day, Allied casualties were over 10,000, with 4,414 confirmed dead. German casualties on that day were about 1,000. In addition, there were about 3,000 civilian casualties. This was the largest amphibious invasion in history, and is considered a key turning point in the story of World War II.

Supreme Allied Commander Dwight D. Eisenhower speaks to paratroopers in England just before they board their airplanes.

Planning for the invasion took more than a year. Four sites were considered for the landing. Two were peninsulas, and were quickly rejected because it would be too easy for German forces to block the Allied advance along a very narrow front. The third, Calais, was the closest to Britain, and was a likely candidate for that reason. The Germans, using the same logic, decided that would be the most likely place for an Allied invasion, so it was by far the heaviest fortified.

Although Normandy was farther away and was also a peninsula, it offered a wider front for an Allied advance as well as the opportunity to take the port of Cherbourg. On the negative side, there were no port facilities in the Normandy peninsula itself, forcing the Allies to develop artificial harbors, known as Mulberry harbors. In addition to the harbors, the Allies also had to develop specialized tanks and numerous landing craft.

Meanwhile, the Allies developed an extensive plan to mislead the Germans as to the date and the location of the planned landings. Among the deceptions, General George S. Patton was given command of the fake First United States Army Group, and through radio traffic, numerous reports, and props built by Hollywood stagehands, helped convince the Germans that the invasion would be in Calais.

The German forces in the West were under the overall command of Field Marshal Gerd for Runstedt, with Field Marshal Erwin Rommel (the "Desert Fox") in command of the Atlantic defenses. Rommel built extensive fortifications all along the French Atlantic coast, including mines, wooden stakes, metal tripods (called "Rommel's Asparagus"), and barbed wire. Unfortunately for the Germans, on D-Day Rommel was back in Germany for his wife's birthday.

Before the actual invasion began, the Allies launched numerous attacks to weaken the German defenders. Bombing raids targeted factories, fuel supplies, and airfields.

The invasion was scheduled to begin on June 5, the date of the full moon, desirable both for illumination and for incoming tides. Forces were already positioned for the invasion, and many ships were already in the English Channel. However, bad weather made the landings impossible. Rather than wait for the next available date, Supreme Allied Commander Dwight D. Eisenhower, in overall command of the invasion, decided that even though weather conditions were still difficult, the invasion would begin the following day.

Rommel believed that the best chance for Germany was to stop any invasion at the shore, so argued that mobile reserves be stationed close to the coast so they could be moved wherever the Allies chose to attack. However, the Nazi high command decided to follow a conventional approach of keeping all the formations in a central position and waiting until it was clear the invasion was underway.

Allied bombers attacked beginning at midnight, but cloud cover made the targets difficult to see. Minesweepers began clearing the way for the invasion fleet shortly thereafter, finishing just after dawn.

The battleship USS Nevada fires on German positions on Utah Beach.

At the same time, troops from the US 82nd and 101st Airborne Divisions began parachuting in to take control of the causeways. However, thick clouds resulted in many paratroopers being dropped far outside their targeted landing zones, and many died.

Allied battleships, cruisers, and destroyers began bombardment of shore defenses beginning shortly after dawn. Although word of the attacks quickly reached German high command, von Runstedt did not believe it was a full invasion and did not react.

The invading forces targeted five sectors, known by the code names Utah, Omaha, Gold, Juno, and Sword. Utah and Omaha were American zones, under the overall command of General Omar Bradley. Gold, Juno and Sword were British and Canadian, under the command of Lieutenant General Sir Miles Dempsey.

At Utah Beach, landing craft of the US 4th Infantry Division were pushed some 2,000 yards south of their intended landing zone by strong currents, but as it happened, there was less opposition at the new invasion site. Although the Utah Beach attackers didn't achieve all their D-Day objectives thanks to the change in landing zones, they got 21,000 troops on shore at the cost of only 197 casualties.

Two divisions, the US 1st Infantry and the 29th Infantry, attacked Omaha Beach, the most heavily defended, only to find that they were facing an entire German division rather than the expected single regiment. Allied bombers, fearful of hitting their own landing craft, delayed releasing their bombs, and many of the German passive defenses were undamaged.

The German forces were located at the top of a cliff and fired relentlessly at the invaders, resulting in over 2,000 American casualties, and a mere 600 men reaching higher ground on the first day.

Commandos from the British 2nd Army attack Juno Beach

At Gold Beach, high winds also made landings difficult, but naval bombardment had also disabled many German fortifications. Juno Beach landings were also delayed, and the infantry arrived before the armor, resulting in heavy casualties. At Sword Beach, mines and other obstacles made clearing the beach both difficult and time consuming, with nearly 3,000 British and Canadian casualties.

Although the Normandy landings did not achieve all their planned goals on the first day, the invasion was an overall success. Continued indecision on the part of the German command delayed any effective response. In addition, the bombing raids and paratroop drops so damaged the transportation network that it would have been difficult under any circumstances for the Germans to respond effectively.

There was much fighting yet to be done, but the Allied foothold on D-Day was the beginning of the liberation of occupied Europe, and a key factor in the eventual Allied victor on the Western Front. Today, many of the battlefield sites have been preserved for the future, and thousands of people visit the area each year.

The immense scope and scale of the Normandy invasion can be seen in this photograph taken a few days after D-Day, as ships put cargo and troops on shore. Barrage balloons float overhead.

A poster for the National Day of Sweden, originally known as Swedish Flag Day.

June 6 Holidays and Celebrations

Engineering Day (Argentina)

In Argentina, Engineering Day is celebrated on June 6, marking the date in 1870 when Luis Augusto Huergo became the first engineer in that country. Interestingly, Engineer's Day in the same country is celebrated on June 16.

Hyeonchung-il (현충일) (South Korea)

Each June 6, South Korea celebrates Memorial Day, honoring the men and women who died in military service during the Korean War and other battles.

Queensland Day (Australia)

The Australian state of Queensland celebrates June 6 to mark the separation of Queensland from New South Wales by order of Queen Victoria. Awards are given to acknowledge the outstanding achievements of Queenslanders.

Russian Language Day (United Nations)

The United Nations Educational, Scientific, and Cultural Organization (UNESCO) sets aside days each year to promote multilingualism and cultural diversity, as well as to promote equal use of all six of the UN's official working languages throughout the organization.

June 6 is Russian Language Day, in honor of the birthday of Russian poet Aleksandr Pushkin, considered the father of modern Russian literature.

Sveriges Nationaldag (Sweden)

The National Day of Sweden is observed each year on June 6. It has been celebrated since 1916 in honor of the foundation of modern Sweden. It is an official public holiday. (Prior to 1983, it was known as *Svenska flaggans dag*, or Swedish Flag Day.)

Teacher's Day (Bolivia)

Many countries set aside a day each year for the appreciation of teachers. In Bolivia, Teacher's Day is June 6.

National Applesauce Cake Day (United States)

In the United States, almost every day of the year is dedicated to a particular food. Sponsored by manufacturers, retailers, farmers, or simply fans, these days are often proclaimed by the President, Congress, state governors, or mayors.

June 6 is National Applesauce Cake Day. In many countries, applesauce is considered a side dish or condiment, but in the United States, applesauce is often served as a dessert, either alone or in the form of applesauce cake.

Christian Feast Days

In *Western Christianity*, saints commemorated on June 6 include Claude the Thaumaturge, Ini Kopuria

(Church of England and Episcopal Church), Mercellin Champagnat, Norbert of Xanten, and Rafael Guízar y Valencia.

In *Eastern Orthodox Christianity*, it is the commemoration of Venerable Bessarion the Wonderworker of Egypt; Saint Hilarion the New; the Virgin-martyrs Archelais, Thecia, and Susanna; Saint Paisius of Uglich; Saint Jonah of Klimetzk; Saint Jonah of Perm; Saint Attalus the Wonderworker; the Martyr Gelasius; and Saint Photius. (These are celebrated on June 19 by "Old Calendarists.")

Other Holidays

Some holidays are simply made up by individuals, companies, or other organizations, and whether they become widely adopted depends on whether people choose to celebrate them. Here are some opportunities to celebrate on June 6.

June 6 is:

- Amateur Radio Military Appreciation Day (ARMAD)
- Atheists Pride Day
- Barricade Day, celebrated by *Les Miserables* fans commemorating the end of the 1832 June Rebellion in France, which figures prominently in the book.
- Drive-In Movie Day
- Yo-Yo Day, in honor of the birthday of yo-yo manufacturer Donald Duncan.

US Navy aircraft attack Japanese cruisers during the Battle of Midway
(Credit: Commander Griffith Bailey Coale, USNR)

What Happened on June 6?

1813 – Battle of Stoney Creek

During the War of 1812, US forces unsuccessfully invaded British Canada. The turning point in that campaign came on June 6, 1813, when a force of 700 British soldiers defeated an American force nearly twice as large near Stoney Creek, Ontario. The battleground is a National Historic Site of Canada, and the battle is reenacted each year on the weekend closest to June 6.

1832 – June Rebellion

The June Rebellion, also known as the Paris Uprising of 1832, was an attempt by anti-monarchists to overthrow the rule of King Louis Philippe I, and took place on June 5-6, 1832. This rebellion plays a prominent role in the novel (and musical and film) Les Misérables by Victor Hugo. Although the rebellion failed, Louis Philippe I was forced to abdicate in 1848, giving rise to the French Second Republic.

1833 – First US President to Ride a Train

On June 6, 1833, US President Andrew Jackson became the first sitting president to ride on a train, going from Ellicott's Mills (modern-day Ellicott City), Maryland, to Baltimore.

1844 – YMCA Founded

On June 6, 1844, George Williams founded the Young Men's Christian Association, commonly known as the YMCA, to promote Christian principles by developing a healthy body, mind, and spirit. The YMCA is headquartered in Geneva, Switzerland, with associations in 125 countries.

1862 – Battle of Memphis

The Battle of Memphis was a naval battle fought on the Mississippi River. Although it was a huge Union victory and resulted in the loss of any Confederate naval presence on the river, Union leaders failed to grasp its importance at the time. Now, it is best known as the last time civilians with no prior military experience were permitted to command ships in combat.

Engraving from the Battle of Memphis (Credit: A. R. Ward)

1889 – Great Seattle Fire

A huge fire destroyed the central business district of Seattle, Washington, on June 6, 1889. Only one person died in the fire, though several others were killed during the cleanup process. Damage was over $20 million, well over $600 million in today's dollars. After the rebuilding, street levels were raised 22 feet, and today tourists can visit the Seattle Underground to see remains of buildings built over after the fire.

1892 – Chicago "L" Begins Operation

The first part of the Chicago "L", for elevated railway, went into paid service on June 6, 1892, when a steam locomotive pulled four coaches carrying 30 people from 39th Street to Congress Street in 14 minutes. The tracks are still used by the Green Line.

1918 – Battle of Belleau Wood

The World War I Battle of Belleau Wood was fought between June 1 and June 26, 1918, eventually resulting in an Allied victory. On June 6, the 3rd Battalion, 5th Marines, fought a battle that resulted in the highest number of casualties in Marine Corps history up to that time. At the beginning of the Marine advance, double Medal of Honor winner Gunnery Sergeant Dan Daly, led his company's advance with the famous words, "Come on, you sons of bitches, do you want to live forever?"

American marines in Belleau Wood (Credit: Georges Scott)

1933 – First Drive-In Theater

The concept of a drive-in movie theater was patented by New Jersey businessman Richard M. Hollingshead, Jr.. He opened his first drive-in on June 6, 1933, in Camden, New Jersey, with the slogan, "The whole family is welcome, regardless of how noisy the children are."

First Drive-In Theater, Camden, New Jersey, 1933

1942 – Battle of Midway

The World War II naval Battle of Midway took place six months after the Japanese attack on Pearl Harbor between June 3 and June 7, 1942, resulting in a decisive American victory. On June 6, US Navy dive bombers sunk four Japanese aircraft carriers and a cruiser.

1946 – NBA Founded

The Basketball Association of America, was founded on June 6, 1946, with eleven teams. In 1949, it merged with its rival the National Basketball League, and changed its name to the National Basketball Association, or NBA.

1982 – First Lebanon War

The 1982 Lebanon War began on June 6, 1982, when Israeli Defense Forces invaded southern Lebanon to counter repeated attacks by the Palestine Liberation Organization (PLO). The war lasted until 1985, and while the PLO was expelled from Lebanon, increased Syrian influence in that country and the rise of Hezbollah made the war a strategic failure for Israel.

1984 – *Tetris* Released

The hugely popular videogame *Tetris*, designed and programmed by Russian designer and engineer Alexey Pajitnov, was first released on June 6, 1984. The game has sold more than 170 million copies to date, although its creator did not receive royalties on his game until 1996.

1985 – Mengele's Remains Discovered

Nazi physician Josef Mengele, known as the Angel of Death for his role in the Auschwitz concentration camp, fled Germany for Argentina following the end of World War II. Although pursued by West Germany, Israel, and other Nazi hunters, he eluded capture. He drowned while swimming in 1979 and was buried under the false name of "Wolfgang Gerhard." He was discovered after interrogation of some of his known associates, and his grave was exhumed on June 6, 1985.

1997 – "Prom Mom" Incident

On June 6, 1997, high school student Melissa Drexler gave birth in a toilet stall during her senior prom, and placed the baby in a plastic bag and put it in the trash, where it was discovered by the school's janitor. She pled guilty to aggravated manslaughter and was sentence to 15 years in prison, but was paroled after a little over three years.

2002 – Eastern Mediterranean Event

On June 6, 2002, a small asteroid impacted Earth's upper atmosphere, and exploded with the force of a 26-kiloton atomic bomb, slightly larger than the Nagasaki bomb. No one was harmed in the explosion, which (unlike an atomic bomb) produced no radioactive fallout.

Who Was Born on June 6?

Acting

Daniel Logan (June 6, 1987 –)

New Zealand actor Daniel Logan is best known for playing the young Boba Fett in *Star Wars Episode II: Attack of the Clones.*

Danny Strong (June 6, 1974 –)

Actor and screenwriter Danny Strong is known for his performances in *Buffy the Vampire Slayer* and *Gilmore Girls,* and wrote the two-part finale to the *Hunger Games* trilogy.

Paul Giamatti (June 6, 1967 –)

Paul Giamatti was nominated for a Golden Globe for the 2004 film *Sideways,* won a Screen Actors Guild Award for *Cinderella Man*, won both an Emmy and a Screen Actors Guild Award for the HBO series *John Adams*, and another Golden Globe for the 2010 film *Barney's Version.*

Max Casella (June 6, 1967 –)

Actor Max Casella first became known for his role as Vinnie on the television series *Doogie Howser, M. D.*, and went on to roles in *The Sopranos* and *Boardwalk Empire*.

Sandra Bernhard (June 6, 1955 –)

Comedienne and actress Sandra Bernhard is known for her biting stand-up act and is on Comedy Central's list of the 100 Greatest Standups of All Time. She has appeared in numerous television shows and films, including *The King of Comedy, Truth or Dare,* and *Roseanne*.

Robert Englund (June 6, 1947 –)

Actor Robert Englund is best known for playing the serial killer Freddy Krueger in the *Nightmare on Elm Street* film franchise.

David Dukes (June 6, 1945 – October 9, 2000)

Character actor David Dukes appeared in 35 films as well as numerous television programs. He starred in the mini-series *The Winds of War* and had recurring roles on *Dawson's Creek*.

Art

John Trumbull (June 6, 1756 – November 10, 1843)

American Revolutionary War era artist John Trumbull is best known for his historical paintings. His 1817 painting *Declaration of Independence* was used for the reverse side of the two-dollar bill.

The painting *Declaration of Independence* by John Trumbull, as shown on the reverse of the US $2 bill

Diego Velázquez (June 6, 1599 [baptized] – August 6, 1660)

Diego Velázquez was one of the most important painters of the Spanish Golden Age, noted particularly for his portraits. His artwork was a model for later realist and impressionist painters, and numerous modern artists have paid tribute to him by recreating some of his famous works.

Portrait of Pope Innocent X by Diego Velázquez, 1650.

Business

Erik Prince (June 6, 1969 –)

Former US Navy SEAL Erik Prince founded the controversial security contractor Blackwater USA.

Kirk Kerkorian (June 6, 1917 – June 15, 2015)

Billionaire businessman Kirk Kerkorian was a major figure in the development of Las Vegas, building the MGM Grand and other casinos, where he became known as the "father of the mega-resort." His charitable works rebuilding northern Armenia after the 1988 earthquake caused him to be named a National Hero of Armenia.

David T. Abercrombie (June 6, 1867 – August 29, 1931)

Outdoorsman and businessman David Abercrombie co-founded the Abercrombie and Fitch clothing brand.

Crime

Arthur Shawcross (June 6, 1945 – November 10, 2008)

Arthur Shawcross, known as the Genesee River Killer, claimed 14 victims in the Rochester, New York, area. Most of his victims were killed following his parole for manslaughter in the death of two children. The controversial parole has been called "one of the most egregious examples of the unwarranted release of a prisoner."

Journalism

Natalie Morales (June 6, 1972 –)

NBC News television journalist Natalie Morales is known as the news anchor for *The Today Show* and has appeared on *Dateline NBC* and *NBC Nightly News*.

Letters

Harvey Fierstein (June 6, 1954 –)

Tony Award winning actor and playwright Harvey Fierstein is best known for the *Torch Song Trilogy, La Cage aux Folles*, and *Kinky Boots*. He was inducted into the American Theater Hall of Fame in 2007.

V. C. Andrews (June 6, 1923 – December 19, 1986)

Victoria C. Andrews is known for her Gothic horror novels, most famously the 1979 best-seller *Flowers in the Attic*.

Thomas Mann (June 6, 1875 – August 12, 1955)

German author Thomas Mann won the 1929 Nobel Prize in Literature. His famous works include *Buddenbrooks, The Magic Mountain*, and *Death in Venice*. He became a US citizen in 1944. During World War II he was an active opponent of Nazism, and made a series of speeches to the German people on the BBC.

Thomas Mann

Eliza Orzeszkowa (June 6, 1841 – May 18, 1910)

Polish novelist Eliza Orzeszkowa was nominated for the Nobel Prize in Literature. She wrote over 30 novels and numerous shorter pieces in her career.

Алекса́ндр Пу́шкин (Aleksandr Pushkin) (June 6 [O.S. May 26, 1799 — February 10 [O.S. January 29], 1837)

Aleksandr Pushkin is considered the founder of modern Russian literature, and many regard him as the greatest poet in that language. His most famous work is the drama Boris Godunov. A member of the Russian nobility, Pushkin was spied on by the Tsar's secret police and fought 29 duels before being fatally wounded.

Pierre Corneille (June 6, 1606 – October 1, 1684)

French tragedian Pierre Corneille, along with his contemporaries Molière and Racine, was one of the three great seventeenth-century French dramatists, best known for his play *Le Cid*.

Military

Nathan Hale (June 6, 1755 – September 22, 1776)

During the American Revolution, Continental Army soldier Nathan Hale volunteered to gather intelligence on the British. He was captured and hanged as a spy. According to a British officer who witnessed the hanging, Hale's last words were, "I only regret that I have but one life to give for my country."

Portrait of Aleksandr Pushkin, Vasily Tropinin, 1827

Music

HyunA (김현아) (June 6, 1992 –)

Korean pop (K-pop) star and dancer Kim Hyuna (stylized as HyunA) gained international fame for her appearance in the video "Gangnam Style," and has has many solo hits including "Bubble Pop" and "Ice Cream."

HyunA at the 2014 Gyeongju Hallyu Dream Concert

Maria Alyokhina (Мари́я Алёхина) (June 6, 1988 –)

Musician and Russian political activist Maria Alyokhina was sentenced to two years' imprisonment for her activities with the punk rock group Pussy Riot.

Jimmy Jam (June 6, 1959 –)

Songwriter, record producer, and keyboard player James Harris, better known as Jimmy Jam, performed with Prince and The Time before partnering with Terry Lewis in producing albums for such artists as Janet Jackson, Mariah Carey, the Spice Girls, George Michael, and many others.

Gary U. S. Bonds (June 6, 1939 –)

Rock and blues singer Gary U. S. Bonds (Gary Anderson) is famous for such hits as "New Orleans" and "Quarter to Three."

Levi Stubbs (June 6, 1936 – October 17, 2008)

Levi Stubbs was known as the lead vocalist of the Four Tops, and provided the voice for "Audrey II," the evil plant in the 1986 film *Little Shop of Horrors*.

Aram Khachaturian (Арам Хачатурян) (June 6, 1903 – May 1, 1978)

Soviet-Armenian composer and conductor Aram Khachaturian is best known for his "Sabre Dance," from the ballet musical *Gayanne*. He composed numerous film scores, including the sound track for the 1954 film *Spartacus*.

Jimmie Lunceford (June 6, 1902 – July 12, 1947)

Jazz saxophonist and bandleader Jimmie Lunceford died after possibly being poisoned by a restaurant owner angry at having to serve an African-American.

Ted Lewis (June 6, 1890 – August 25, 1971)

Bandleader Ted Lewis, known as "Mr. Entertainment," made famous the catchphrase "Is everybody happy?"

Politics

Eric Cantor (June 6, 1963 –)

Republican Eric Cantor served as House Majority Leader from 2011 to 2014, and was the highest-ranking Jewish member of Congress in its history. He was defeated in an upset election in 2014 and subsequently resigned.

Ted Lewis

Roy Innis (June 6, 1934 –)

Civil rights activist Roy Innis has been the chair of the Congress of Racial Equality (CORE) since 1968.

Sukarno (June 6, 1901 – June 21, 1970)

A leader in the Indonesian struggle for independence from the Netherlands, Sukarno was appointed as president of the newly free state. Governing with a combination of Marxism, nationalism, and Islam that he called "guided democracy," he was made President for Life until overthrown in 1967, and spent the remainder of his life under house arrest.

Italo Balbo (June 6, 1896 – June 28, 1940)

Italian fascist Italo Balbo was considered the heir apparent to dictator Benito Mussolini, though he opposed both anti-Jewish laws and the Italian alliance with Adolf Hitler. He was shot down by friendly fire over Tobruk while serving as governor of Italian Libya.

Science

Richard Smalley (June 6, 1943 – October 28, 2005)

Nobel Prize-winning chemist Richard Smalley discovered a new form of carbon, buckminsterfullerine (buckyballs), a key development in the field of nanotechnology.

Regiomontanus (June 6, 1436 – July 6, 1476)

Regiomontanus (Johannes von Konigsberger) was an astronomer, an astrologer, a mathematician, an instrument maker, and a Catholic bishop. He was internationally famous in his lifetime, making contributions to trigonometry, algebra, and astronomy. He influenced the work of Copernicus, who first demonstrated that the Earth revolved around the Sun.

Sports

Cam Neely (June 6, 1965 –)

Cam Neely was inducted into the Hockey Hall of Fame following a 13-year career with the Vancouver Canucks and Boston Bruins.

Ahmed Johnson (June 6, 1963 –)

Professional wrestler Ahmed Johnson was the first African-American to win a WWF singles championship.

Dave Schultz (June 6, 1959 – January 26, 1996)

Olympic gold medalist and world champion wrestler Dave Schultz, along with his brother Mark, won more NCAA, U. S. Open, World, and Olympic titles than any American brother combination in history. He was murdered by millionaire heir John du Pont, following events portrayed in the 2014 film *Foxcatcher*.

Björn Borg (June 6, 1956 –)

World champion tennis player Björn Borg won 11 Grand Slam singles titles and set numerous career records, including being the first player to earn more than $1 million in prize money during a single season.

Björn Borg (Photo: C. Thomas)

Tommie Smith (June 6, 1944 –)

American track and field athlete and football player Tommie Smith won the 200-meter dash gold medal in the 1968 Summer Olympics, breaking the 20-second barrier for the first time. While atop the medal platform, he gave a Black Power salute, which resulted in controversy.

Olympians John Carlos (left) and Tommie Smith (atop the podium).
Smith is giving the Black Power salute as a protest against racial
discrimination. (Photo: Angelo Cozzi, Mondadori Publishers)

Eddie Giacomin (June 6, 1939 –)

Ice hockey goaltender Eddie Giacomin played for the New York Rangers and Detroit Red Wings during his 19-year career.

Bill Dickey (June 6, 1907 – November 12, 1993)

New York Yankees catcher Bill Dickey played for 19 seasons, and became manager of the Yankees upon his retirement in 1946. As a player, his team won eight World Series championships, and as a manager and coach won six more. He was elected to the Baseball Hall of Fame in 1954.

Bill Dickey's 1933 Goudey baseball card

Who Died on June 6?

Acting, Film, and Television

Esther Williams (August 8, 1921 — June 6, 2013)

Competitive swimmer and actress Esther Williams appeared in a number of "aquamusicals" in the 1940s and 1950s, including "Million Dollar Mermaid."

Esther Williams from the trailer to *Dangerous When Wet* (1953)

Anne Bancroft (September 17, 1931 — June 6, 2005)

Actress Anne Bancroft won an academy award, two Golden Globes, two Tonys and two Emmys. Her best known films include *The Miracle Worker* (1962), *The Graduate* (1967), and *The Turning Point* (1977).

Jack Haley (August 10, 1897 — June 6, 1979)

Actor, singer, and dancer Jack Haley is best remembered for his portrayal of the Tin Man in the 1939 film *The Wizard of Oz*.

From left to right: Jack Haley, Ray Bolger, Judy Garland, and Bert Lahr in a publicity still from *The Wizard of Oz*.

Louis Lumière (October 5, 1864– June 6, 1948)

The Lumière brothers, Auguste and Louis, were the first filmmakers in history. Unlike the Edison kinetoscope, which could be viewed by only one person at a time, they invented the cinematograph, which could be viewed by multiple people at the same time. They made what is considered the first motion picture in history.

The first advertising poster for a motion picture, 1895.

Lillian Russell (December 4, 1860 — June 6, 1922)

Lillian Russell was one of the most famous American actresses and singers of the late 19th and early 20th centuries. She was the mistress of Diamond Jim Brady, and was an advocate of women's suffrage.

Lillian Russell, 1889 (Photo: Jake Falk)

Animals

Shrek (November 27, 1994 — June 6, 2011)

New Zealand sheep Shrek became internationally famous when he avoided being caught and shorn for six years. His shearing was broadcast on New Zealand television, and his fleece contained enough wool to make 20 large men's suits.

Shrek the Sheep prior to shearing

Business

J. Paul Getty (December 15, 1892 — June 6, 1976)

Founder of the Getty Oil Company, J. Paul Getty was named the world's richest private citizen in the 1966 Guinness Book of World Records. His collection of art and antiquities is featured in the J. Paul Getty Museum in Los Angeles, California.

Louis Chevrolet (December 25, 1878 — June 6, 1941)

Race car driver Louis Chevrolet founded the Chevrolet Motor Car Company in 1911. He competed in the Indianapolis 500 four times, coming in second in 1919 and third in 1920. He was named to the International Motorsports Hall of Fame in 1992.

Louis Chevrolet

Letters

Vincent Bugliosi (August 18, 1934 — June 6, 2015)

Attorney and author Vincent Bugliosi was a prosecutor in Los Angeles. He wrote numerous true-crime best-sellers including 1974's *Helter Skelter*, about the Manson murders, which he prosecuted.

Bertram Chandler (March 28, 1912 — June 6, 1984)

Australian merchant marine captain A. Bertram Chandler wrote over 40 novels and 200 short stories while sailing the world in vessels ranging from tramp steamers to troop ships.

Kenneth Rexroth (December 22, 1905 — June 6, 1982)

Poet Kenneth Rexroth was called the "Father of the Beats" by *Time* magazine, although he did not consider himself a Beat poet. He is an important figure in the San Francisco Renaissance poetry movement.

Military

William Quantrill (July 31, 1837 — June 6, 1865)

Confederate guerrilla leader William Quantrill is remembered for raiding the Union town of Lawrence, Kansas, and the subsequent massacre of its citizens in 1863.

The Lawrence Massacre, led by William Quantrill.

Music

Marvin Isley (August 18, 1953 — June 6, 2010)

Marvin Isley was the youngest member of the music group The Isley Brothers.

Stan Getz (February 2, 1927 — June 6, 1991)

Jazz tenor saxophonist Stan Getz is best known for his worldwide hit single "The Girl from Ipanema." He won numerous Grammy Awards and is a member of the Jazz Hall of Fame.

Philosophy

Jeremy Bentham (February 15 [O.S. February 4], 1748 — June 6, 1832)

Philosopher and jurist Jeremy Bentham is best known as the founder of utilitarianism, a philosophical principle that argues that the measure of right and wrong is "the greatest happiness of the greatest number." Many of his ideas, including the separation of church and state, equal rights for women, and the abolition of slavery, once radical, are now mainstream..

Jeremy Bentham, by Henry William Pickersgill

Politics

Robert F. Kennedy (November 20, 1925 — June 6, 1968)

Brother of US President John F. Kennedy, Robert (Bobby) Kennedy served as a Senator and as Attorney General before running for President in 1968. He was shot by Sirhan Sirhan on June 5 following his victory in the California Democratic primary election and died the following day.

Robert F. Kennedy

John A. Macdonald (January 11, 1815 — June 6, 1891)

Known as the "Father of Confederation," John A. Macdonald was a key figure in the creation of modern Canada and served for 19 years as its first prime minister.

Patrick Henry (May 29, 1736 — June 6, 1799)

American founding father Patrick Henry was active in the independence movement in Virginia and afterwards served as Governor of Virginia. He is famous for his "Give me liberty or give me death!" speech, helping to pass a resolution to provide Virginian troops to the American Revolutionary War.

Patrick Henry, by George Bagby Matthews

Science, Medicine and Technology

Carl Jung (July 26, 1875 — June 6, 1961)

Swiss psychiatrist Carl Jung developed analytical psychology, and created such fundamental concepts as the archetype, the collective unconscious, and the complex.

Robert Stirling (October 25, 1790 — June 6, 1878)

Scottish clergyman Robert Stirling is known as the inventor of the Stirling engine, a high efficiency closed-cycle regenerative heat engine. Although it lost out to the steam engine, its approach is compatible with alternative and renewable energy sources and is currently receiving new interest.

June:
The Sixth Month

And what is so rare as a day in June?
Then, if ever, come perfect days;
Then Heaven tries earth if it be in tune,
And over it softly her warm ear lays.

       — *"An April Day," Henry Wadsworth Longfellow*

In the Julian and Gregorian calendars, June is the sixth month of the year. It's one of the four months that have only 30 days. No months start on the same day of the week as June, an oddity shared only by May. However, June ends on the same day of the week as March in both common and leap years.

In the Northern Hemisphere, June is the month with the longest daylight hours; in the Southern Hemisphere, it's the one with the shortest, equivalent to December. The meteorological summer begins June 21 (the Summer Solstice) in the Northern Hemisphere; the meteorological winter begins on the same day in the Southern Hemisphere (the Winter Solstice).

The English name of June takes its name from the Latin *Iunius.* The poet Ovid gives two theories for the origin of the name. The first is that June is named for the Roman goddess Juno, wife of Jupiter and queen of the gods. The second is that the name comes from the Latin word *iuniores* ("younger ones"), and that the previous month of May comes from maiores ("elders")

As the early Roman calendar started its new year in March, June was originally the fourth month of the year. It's uncertain when the Romans switched the new year to January, but it may have been as late as 153 BCE.

June in Other Cultures

The month of June has different names in different languages. Some nations use calendars other than the Gregorian, and their months may overlap with June. In lunar-based calendars, such as Islam, months move through the seasons. Still, many languages often have a word for *June* itself.

Albanian: Qershor

Arabic (Egyptian, Sudanese, Moroccan): يونيو (*yūniyū*)

Arabic (Levantine): حزيران(*ḥuzayrān*)

Arabic (Libyan): الصيف (*al-sayf*)

Arabic (Algerian): جوان (*Juwān*)

Azerbaijani: İyun

Basque: Ekain

Bulgarian: юни (*juni*)

Chinese: 六月 (Cantonese: *luhkyuht*; Mandarin: *liùyuè*; Taiwanese: *lak-goeh*)

Corsican: Chjugnu

Czech: červen

Finnish: Kesäkuu

French: Juin

German, Norwegian: Juni

Greek: Ιούνιος (*Ioúnios*)

Hebrew: יוני (*yûnî*)

Hindi: जून (*jūn*)

Hungarian: Június

Irish (Gaelic): Meitheamh mí an Mheithimh

Italian: Giugno

Japanese (traditional calendar): 六月 (*rokugatsu*); 水無月 (*minaduki*)

Korean: 유월 (*yuweol*)

Lithuanian: Birželis

Maori: Pipiri

Old English: Sēremōnaþ

Polish: Czerwiec

Russian: июнь (*ijun'*)

Sesotho: Phupjane

Spanish: Junio

Swedish, Swahili: Juni

Thai: Mithunayon

Vietnamese: 腖𦝃 (tháng sáu)

Welsh: Mehefin

June Brides and Other Sayings and Superstitions

June is the most popular month for weddings, followed by August. There are a number of sayings and superstitions about June brides and June weddings.

"A June bride is joyful, jubilant, and jolly well jovial."

"A June bride will be impetuous, and generous."

"Married in the month of roses (June), life will be one long honeymoon."

"Marry when June roses grow, over land and sea you'll go."

"When you marry in June, you'll be a bride all your life." (from the song *June Bride*.)

Why such an emphasis on June? Some say it's in honor of
Juno, the goddess of marriage. Others suggest it's because
back in Medieval days, people would usually have their
(yes) annual bath in May, so they'd still be relatively fresh
by June. This may also explain the custom of the bridal
bouquet.

According to superstition, May is the most unlucky month
for marriages, but in ancient Rome the "inauspicious"
period ran from May 15 to June 15. The high priestess of
Jupiter told the poet Ovid to delay his daughter's
wedding until after that date.

There are also some June proverbs for farmers.

"A calm June puts the farmer in tune."

"June damp and warm, does the farmer no harm."

April, by Hans Thoma

June Symbols

Birthstone Pearl, moonstone, or alexandrite.

Pearl

Moonstone

Michael Dobson

Alexandrite

Birth Flowers Rose and Honeysuckle

Roses, by Vincent van Gogh

June Events

Honorary Months

Presidents, Congresses, and nations around the world issue proclamations recognizing particular months to honor certain causes. These events generally fall in June, though honorary months do come and go. Holidays established by states and nonprofit organizations are listed if verified. If not otherwise specified, all months are US.

Sarah Vaughn

- African-American Music Appreciation Month
- Bicycle Month (May 25 to June 25) (Canada)
- Caribbean American Heritage Month
- Crop over (Barbados), celebrated until the first Monday in August.
- Gay and Lesbian Pride Month (US)
- Great Outdoors Month (US)
- National Smile Month (UK)
- National Oceans Month (United States)
- Season of Emancipation (June 64 to August 23) (Barbados)

Moveable and Multi-Day Events

Some events take place over a specific week or time period. Start and finish dates may vary from year to year. Some events occur on different days each year (such as "fourth Saturday of a month"). The following events sometimes occur on June 6.

First Monday
- June Holiday (*Lá Saoire i mí Mheitheamh*) (Republic of Ireland)
- Queen's Official Birthday (New Zealand, Cook Islands, Western Australia)
- Western Australia Day

First Friday
- Labour Day (Bahamas)
- National Doughnut Day (United States)

First Saturday
- Drawing Day / Pencil Day
- National Trails Day (United States)
- Saiō Matsuri (Meiwa, Mie, Japan)

First Sunday
- Armed Forces Day (Canada)
- Children's Awareness Memorial Day
- Father's Day (Lithuania, Switzerland)
- Mother's Day (France, only if Pentecost occurs on the last Sunday in May, when the holiday is typically held.)
- National Cancer Survivors Day (United States)
- Teacher's Day (Hungary)
- The Seamen's Day (Iceland)

June Zodiac Signs

From the perspective of someone on Earth, the Sun appears to move through the sky throughout the year, along a path astronomers call the *ecliptic plane*. The ecliptic plane is divided into twelve constellations, known as the zodiac, based on traditionally observed patterns of stars. On your birthday, you can't see your constellation, because it's in the daytime sky.

The zodiac was first developed by Babylonian astronomers about 2,500 years ago. Because they were unaware that the Earth wobbles like a spinning top (known as *precession*), they didn't make allowance for the fact that the Sun's path through the zodiac changes over time.

That means there are now two sets of dates for your birth sign. The *tropical dates* are the original Babylonian dates; the *sidereal dates* tell you where the Sun actually appears as it moves along its annual path.

For June 6, the tropical sign is Gemini and the sidereal sign is Taurus.

Taurus

Tropical April 21 to May 21
Sidereal May 16 to June 15

The astrological sign of Taurus (the Bull) originated in ancient Mesopotamia, who called it the "Bull of Heaven," and believed it to be a symbol of strong will, perseverance, and determination. The Egyptians knew it as Hathor (the Cow Goddess), who was the goddess of beauty, love, and happiness. That's why Roman astrologers said that Taurus was ruled by Venus, their goddess of beauty.

In astrology, Taurus is an Earth sign, compatible with Cancer, Capricorn, and Pisces. Taureans are supposed to be headstrong, powerful, and hard-working.

Gemini

Tropical May 22 to June 21
Sidereal June 16 to July 15

According to Greek mythology, Leda, wife of the King of Sparta, gave birth to Helen of Troy and Clytemnestra. The god Zeus, disguised as a swan, seduced her after she had already lain with her husband on the same night. This resulted in two eggs, which hatched to become the twins Castor and Pollux. Castor's father was the King of Sparta, but Pollux was the son of Zeus and therefore immortal. When Castor died, Pollux shared his immortality, so that they could divide their time between Hades and Olympus. They were enshrined in the Zodiac as the constellation Gemini, the Twins.

In astrology, Gemini is an air sign, ruled by Mercury, compatible with Libra, Aquarius, and Aries. Geminis are supposed to be communicative, flexible, intellectual, and curious, but prone to fickleness and easily distracted.

Illustration by Edward Penfield

What Day of the Week is June 6?

On what day of the week does June 6 fall?

Surprisingly, this isn't an easy question. Because the calendar year is 365 days long (366 in leap years), it doesn't divide evenly by the seven days of the week.

Also, the Earth goes around the Sun in about 365-1/4 days, so a calendar tends to drift over time. That's why the same date falls on different weekdays in different years.

This is made even more complicated by a change in calendars that took place in 1582. Our modern calendar has its roots in ancient Rome, in a calendar reform conducted by Julius Caesar. Caesar commissioned mathematicians to attack the problem, and they came up with the idea of leap years, and thus standardized the calendar for centuries to come. This was called the Julian calendar.

Over time, however, the small errors in Caesar's calculation compounded. That's why Pope Gregory XIII commissioned the Gregorian calendar, used in most of the world today. Some countries converted in 1582, when the calendar was first developed; some converted later; other still haven't changed.

Gregorian and Julian aren't the only types of calendars. The Hebrew year, the Islamic year, and many other calendars are used in different parts of the world and among different people.

You can convert Gregorian dates to other calendars, including the Hebrew calendar, the Islamic calendar, and even the Mayan calendar by visiting the Fourmilab Calendar Converter at http://www.fourmilab.ch/documents/calendar/.

Chinese calendar systems are quite complex and have changed several times; a full discussion is far beyond the scope of this book. If you're interested, you can find information here: http://www.hermetic.ch/cal_stud/chinese_cal.htm.

On Names and Dates

Historians use "CE" (Common Era) and "BCE" (Before the Common Era) instead of the more common "AD" (Anno Domini, or Year of Our Lord) and "BC" (Before Christ), reflecting the fact that the year-numbering system established by the Gregorian calendar is used throughout the world in many countries not culturally Christian.

The CE/BCE designation dates back to at least 1708, and has been adopted as a standard by the United Nations and the Universal Postal Union. Because this series of books covers events and people of all nations and cultures, we use the CE/BCE terms.

The abbreviation "O.S." ("Old Style") on some dates refers to the fact that the Russian Empire did not switch from the Julian to the Gregorian calendar at the same time as the rest of Europe, and therefore some figures and events have two dates.

Also, in the Julian calendar in England in the 16th century, the year began on March 25 rather than January 1. To avoid confusion with Gregorian dates, dates between January and March were often written using both years.

People and events whose original names are not in the Western alphabet have their native names (where possible) in the appropriate script shown in parenthesis. If you are using an e-reader to access an electronic version of this book, all characters don't always display on all devices.

A 50-year brass perpetual calendar.

Cartoon by John T. McCutcheon

Copyright, Credit, and Contact

Follow Us

Our blog Dobson's Improbable History (http://improbhistory.blogspot.com) features short articles on events and people associated with each day, and updates several times each week. You can also get a daily "What Happened In History" message and all the latest Timespinner Press news by following us on Facebook at https://www.facebook.com/TimespinnerPress. Our Twitter feed @SidewiseThinker links you to all our News of the Day.

Contact Us

Find an error or a format problem? Want information about the series, about us, or about when the volume for your special day might be available? Please email us at editor@timespinnerpress.com. (We also take requests if your special day isn't yet complete. Please give us at least six weeks' notice if possible.)

Dedication

In addition to the many other reasons why June 6 is a very special day, it's also the birthday of my brother, Patrick Dobson, to whom this volume is dedicated.

Sources

We owe a great debt to Wikipedia, which is our first stop for research. We attempt to make independent confirmation of all important dates and facts through a variety of other sources. Other sources we frequently use include the Library of Congress; "on this day" listings from *Encyclopedia Britannica*, the *New York Times*, and the BBC; Omniglot for the names of months in other languages; *Chase's Calendar of Events*; and, of course, the always essential Google.

All art and photographs are either in the public domain, used under a Creative Commons license, or with a "fair use" justification, and most frequently come from Wikimedia Commons and the Library of Congress Prints and Photographs Division.

Attribution is provided where possible, or as requested by the copyright owner, or when there is particular historical significance, listed below. For information about any particular illustration or photograph, please contact us.

Credits

* The illustration of the month of June used on the back cover and as the frontispiece is from the French Gothic illuminated manuscript *Les Très Riches Heures du duc de Berry* by the Limbourg Brothers, Jean Colombe, and an intermediate painter whose name is lost to history.
* The cover photograph, titled "Into the Jaws of Death—US Troops Wading Through Water and Nazi Gunfire," was taken on June 6, 1944 by US Coast Guard Chief Photographer's Mate Robert F. Sargent, and is from the collection of the Franklin D. Roosevelt Library, part of the National Archives and Records Administration. As a work created by an employee of the United States federal government, it is in the public domain. (NARA ARC 195515).

- The painting of Patrick Henry before the Virginia House of Burgesses was painted by Peter F. Rothermel in 1851, and is in the public domain because its copyright is expired.

- The US Navy photograph of US troops nearing Utah Beach is in the public domain as a work created by an employee or sailor of the US government.

- The US Army photograph of Gen. Dwight D. Eisenhower speaking to paratroopers is in the public domain as a work created by an employee or soldier of the US government.

- The photograph of British forces attacking Juno Beach is in the public domain as a work created by the government of the United Kingdom taken prior to June 1, 1957.

- The photograph of landing ships putting cargo ashore on one of the invasion beaches a few days after D-Day is in the public domain as a work created by an employee or soldier of the US government.

- The 1916 poster celebrating Swedish Flag Day is in the public domain because its copyright has expired.

- The drawing of the attack on Japanese cruisers during the Battle of Midway is by Commander Griffith Bailey Coale, USNR, and is part of the US Navy Art Collection. It is in the public domain as work of a sailor or employee of the US Navy, created as part of that person's official duties.

- The engraving of the Battle of Memphis is by A. R. Ward. It is in the public domain because its copyright has expired.

- The drawing "American Marines in Belleau Wood (1918)" is by Georges Scott and was originally published in the French magazine *Illustrations*. It is in the public domain because its copyright has expired.

- The photograph of the first drive-in movie theater was originally published in *Electronics* magazine, Vol. 6, No. 8, August 1933 issue. It is in the public domain because it was published in the United States between 1923 and 1963, and although there may or may not have been a copyright notice, the copyright was not renewed.

- The back of the US $2 bill is in the public domain as an image of paper currency not suitable for or intended to be used for counterfeit or fraudulent purpose.

- The 1650 portrait of Pope Innocent X by Diego Velázquez is in the public domain because its copyright has expired.

- The 1929 Nobel Prize publicity photograph of Thomas Mann is in the public domain because it is a journalistic work created before 1969.

- The 1827 portrait of Aleksandr Pushkin by Vasily Tropinin is in the public domain because its copyright has expired.

- The 2014 photograph of HyunA at the Gyeongju Hallyu Dream Concert was taken by "doolki," and is used here under CC BY-SA 4.0.

- The 1951 publicity photo of Ted Lewis is in the public domain because it was published in the US between 1923 and 1977 without a copyright notice. Traditionally, publicity photographs are not copyrighted.

- The 2011 photograph of Björn Borg was taken by C. Thomas, and is used here under CC BY-SA 2.0

- The 1968 photograph of Olympic Gold Medalist Tommie Smith giving the Black Power salute during the medal presentation is in the public domain in Italy, where it was first published. It is uncertain whether there is a US copyright, and if so, its use here is permitted under "fair use" rules because it illustrates an important historical moment, no free equivalents are available, and the size and resolution are too low to facilitate the production of counterfeit goods. The photograph was taken by Angelo Cozzi for Mondadori Publishers.

- The 1933 Goudey baseball card of Bill Dickey is in the public domain because it was published in the US between 1923 and 1977 either without a copyright notice, or if there was a copyright, it was not renewed.

- The trailer screenshot of Esther Williams in the 1953 film *Dangerous When Wet* is in the public domain because it was published in the US between 1923 and 1977 without a copyright notice.

- The 1895 film poster advertising the Lumière brothers film *L'Arroseur Arrosé* is in the public domain because its copyright has expired.

- The 1889 portrait photograph of Lillian Russell is by Benjamin "Jake" Falk. It is in the public domain because its copyright has expired.

- The photograph of Shrek the Sheep is used here under "fair use" rules because it illustrates an important historical moment, no free equivalents are available, and the size and resolution are too low to facilitate the production of counterfeit goods. No copyright information is available.

- The photograph of Louis Chevrolet is from the George Grantham Bain Collection, Library of Congress (ggbain. 22926). It is in the public domain because of the terms under which the Library purchased the collection in 1948.

- "The Destruction of the City of Lawrence, Kansas, and the Massacre of Its Inhabitants by the Rebel Guerrillas, August 21, 1863," originally appeared in *Harper's Weekly*, Vol. 7, No. 349, dated September 5, 1863. It is in the public domain because its copyright has expired.

- The detail from the portrait of Jeremy Bentham by Henry William Pickersgill is in the public domain because the painter died in 1875 and any copyright has expired.

- The 1964 photograph of Robert F. Kennedy in the White House Cabinet Room was taken by White House photographer Yoichi R. Okamoto. It is in the public domain as a work created by an employee of the US federal government.

- The circa 1891 portrait of Patrick Henry by George Bagby Matthews is in the public domain because its copyright has expired.

- The painting *Juni* is from the calendar book *Festkalender* by Hans Thoma. It is in the pubic domain because its copyright has expired.

- The photo of a pearl necklace is by "Anna reg," taken from Wikimedia Commons and used here under CC BY-SA 3.0.

- The photograph of a Brazilian moonstone is by Didier Descouens, taken from Wikimedia Commons and used here under CC BY-SA 4.0.

- The photograph of alexandrite under ultraviolet light is by Parent Géry, taken from Wikimedia Commons and used here because the creator has dedicated the rights to the public domain under CC0 1.0.

- The painting *Roses* by Vincent Van Gogh can be found in the collection of the National Gallery of Art, Washington, DC. The image is in the public domain because its copyright has expired.

- The illustration of honeysuckle originally appeared in the book *American Homes and Gardens*, published by Munn & Co., New York, in 1905. It is in the public domain because its copyright has expired. The image was taken from Flickr's The Commons.

- The 1946 photograph of Sarah Vaughn was taken by William P. Gottlieb, and is part of the William P. Gottlieb Collection of jazz photographs at the Library of Congress. In accordance with the wishes of Gottlieb, the photographs in the collection entered into the public domain in 2010.

- The 1906 automobile calendar is by Edward Penfield, and is in the collection of the Library of Congress Prints and Photographs Division. It is in the public domain because its copyright has expired.

- The 50-year perpetual calendar photograph is in the public domain.

- The cartoon by John T. McCutcheon is from his 1905 collection *The Mysterious Stranger and Other Cartoons by John T. McCutcheon*. It is in the public domain because its copyright has expired.

License Description and Terms

Aside from material purely in the public domain, photographs and other material in this book are used under specific licenses permitting free use, usually with an attribution requirement. For full text and terms of these licenses, click or enter the appropriate links below. If you believe there is an error in the copyright status or attribution of any of these images, please email us.

- Creative Commons Attribution 2.0 Generic (CC-BY 2.0): http://creativecommons.org/licenses/by/2.0/deed.en

- Creative Commons Attribution-Share Alike 3.0 Generic (CC-BY-SA 3.0): http://creativecommons.org/licenses/by-sa/3.0/

- Creative Commons Attribution-Share Alike 2.5 Generic (CC-BY-SA 2.5): http://creativecommons.org/licenses/by-sa/2.5/deed.en

- Creative Commons Attribution-Share Alike 2.0 Generic (CC-BY-SA 2.0): http://creativecommons.org/licenses/by/2.0/deed.en

- Creative Commons Attribution-Share Alike 1.0 Generic (CC-BY-SA 1.0): http://creativecommons.org/licenses/by-sa/1.0/deed.en

- CC0 1.0 Universal (CC0 1.0) Public Domain Dedication (CC0 1.0) http://creativecommons.org/publicdomain/zero/1.0/deed.en

- GNU Free Documentation License (GFDL): http://en.wikipedia.org/wiki/Wikipedia:Text_of_the_GNU_Free_Documentation_License

Timespinner
Press

Other Books from Timespinner Press

The Story of a Special Day
Michael Dobson

A series of (eventually) 366 volumes covering everything that
happened on your special day! Events, births, deaths, quotes,
holidays, and much more. It's like a birthday card they'll never
throw away!

US$7.95 print / US$2.99 ebook.

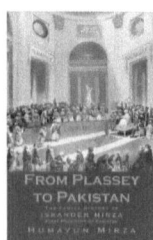

From Plassey to Pakistan
Humayun Mirza

The history of British Colonial India and the
formation of Pakistan from the unique
perspective of the son of Pakistan's first president
and last of the royal line of Bengal, Bihar, and
Orissa!

US$27.95 print

A Whole New Navy: America's War in the Pacific
Miles Durr

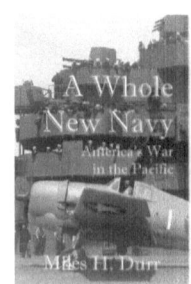

The most comprehensive and detailed description
of America's naval war in the Pacific ever—every
battle, every ship, every task force and every task
group from Pearl Harbor through the Japanese
surrender!

US$29.95 print